FOR A PUN TIME CALL SMITTY

FOR A PUN TIME CALL SMITTY

Timothy "Smitty" Smith
Louisville, KY

FOR A PUN TIME CALL SMITTY
This is a work of non-fiction. All puns and jokes
in this book are original works of the author. Any
similarities to other works are coincidental.

FOR A PUN TIME CALL SMITTY © 2020 Timothy Smith

All rights reserved. No part of this publication may be recorded,
stored in a retrieval system, or transmitted in any form or by
any means, electronic, mechanical, photocopying, recording, or
otherwise, without prior written permission from the publisher.

ISBN: 978-0-578-72019-7

Published by Timothy Smith
Louisville, KY

Printed in the United States of America
First Edition August 2020

Cover Design by: Make Your Mark Publishing Solutions
Interior Layout by: Make Your Mark Publishing Solutions
Editing: Make Your Mark Publishing Solutions
Cover Art and Illustrations: Randy Gray

Contents

Dedication vii

Bad Pickup Lines 1

Yo Mama Jokes 13

The Rest of Yo Family Jokes 25

Miscellaneous Jokes 57

Acknowledgements 89

Dedication

This book is dedicated to my late mother, Dolores Smith, who, through her own challenges, taught me to believe in myself and never give up. I love you, Mom!

BAD PICKUP LINES

Call me the Tampa Buccaneers because I want you to be my "Bay!"

I want to spend "Minute by Minute" with you because you "Doobie" looking good!

Is your heart frozen? Because you are cold blooded!

Do you shoot craps? Because looking at you is like a "pair a dice!"

I'm gonna call you Delta because you so fly!

I just got a library card because I be checking you out every day!

Why don't you tutor me in your math class so I can get them digits!

Let me take you shoe shopping so you can be my sole mate!

I'm going to change my name to Orville Redenbacher because it could be on and poppin'!

Ladies' response to a bad pickup line: Why don't you act like a terrible DJ and get outta here with all that noise!

Let me find the phone number to the Goodwill Store pickup because you got junk in your trunk!

Why don't you be like a Monopoly game and give me a chance!

Call me Ray because I'm looking at sunshine!

You are like a good KFC cook because you got some nice legs!

Throw something on the floor so you can take a trip with me!

Throw something in the street so we can take a road trip!

Is your name Pam Grier? Because I wanna meet you somewhere for coffee!

Let's grow a garden together so we can turnip!

I'm gonna buy a football so I can kick it with you!

You are like a traffic signal on red; you can stop traffic!

Let me take you home like *The Brady Bunch* so you can "Cialis" working!

Can I call you honey? Because I wanna "bee" your man!

You're so fine, forget about your sign; what's your signature?

You're so fine, I wanna write you a ticket myself and then throw it out in court!

I'm going to grill out for you because I will gladly give you some more of my ribs!

Can I be your lawyer? I want to plead guilty for you and sentence you to life with me!

You're like Icy Hot because you're cool as hell!

I almost called you Snoop Dogg because you're definitely smokin'!

You're like Twitter; I'd follow you anywhere!

Can I take you deer hunting? Because you are dressed to kill, doe!

You're like the American flag; you've got my attention!

Let me be your warden because you are killing 'em!

I smell rain because you are definitely thunder!

Can I call you Slinky? Because you got me sprung!

You're so fine, I would sleep on your shoes because you got me head over heels!

You're like a dictionary with blank pages because words can't describe you!

Get somebody to call a tow truck because I want to hook up with ya!

Give me your shoulder blades so I can *always* have your back!

Girl, you are like me wearing my little brother's suit; you are so tight!

Do you own a sandpaper company? Because you can make my jagged edges smooth!

Can I be your Geico commercial pig so "weeeeeeeee" can hang out?

Have you seen my other shoe? Because I'm looking for my sole mate!

You are like a stranded motorist in the middle of nowhere; you got a hell of a walk!

You're like the WWE because you're slammin'!

Let me take you to a haunted house so you can be my boo thang!

I was like a bad actor when I first saw you; I had to do a double take!

I'm going to take away your driver's license because you are driving me crazy!

Can I glue my picture on your forehead so I can stay on your mind?

A lady's response to a bad pickup line from a guy: Why don't you act like a frat brother and get to stepping!

Is your name Honeycomb? Because you need to "bee" with me!

Call me calculator because you can always count on me!

You're like my grandmama's old screen door; you're definitely slammin'!

I wanna be your employer; you can come "t-werk" for me anytime!

You're so fine, there ought to be only one season all year long because I'd "fall" for you every time!

You're like someone who bumped into the DJ's table; my heart skipped a beat when I saw you!

I want to meet your daddy so I can have him practice giving you away!

You're like a barren tree; I'd never "leaf" you!

You are like Seiko, Citizen, and Timex because I can watch you all day!

You're like a lost wallet full of money; I've been looking for you all day!

Do you like chromosomes? Because you are wearing them "genes"!

Let me take you on a trip to Viagra Falls for a pick me up!

Can I be your bubble gum? Because you can have me wrapped around your little finger!

Can I be your Muhammad Ali? Because you're a knockout!

Just call me Cyclops because I got my eye on you!

You got me over here like a ghost because I wanna be your boo!

Just give me all of your credit cards and cash so you'll never be "a loan!"

Make like a binary code and give me those digits!

I want to take you to the Maury show so I *can* be the father!

I want to be like your daddy when you did something very bad and take you out!

You're like a light switch in a dark room with a promiscuous boy because you got it going on!

Let me put an Uber sign on my car because I want to take you home!

Do you like soccer? Because I want to kick it with you!

Go home and pour some ice in your bathtub because I'll drink your bath water!

I'm going to call you Venus and Serena because you're causing a racket up in here!

You're so smart, someone should put your life on *Jeopardy*!

You must be a Siamese twin because I never want to leave your side!

You better call George Jetson because I can see us in the future!

Let me go buy a stroller so you can be my baby!

Don't call me Campbell's because I'm not souped!

Let me put a calendar page on the bottom of our shoes so we can go out on a date!

I hope you got a good lawyer because you're killing 'em!

Why don't you be like B-O-L-O-G-N-A and tell me your first and second name!

I want you to have that puzzled look because I can see us together in the near future!

Your name must be Oxymoron because you look awful good!

I want to invite you as a guest to a potato cooking party because you're a-peel-ing!

I wanna be your Spanx so I can hug you all day long!

You're so fine, you're like a fish that broke loose from the line: off da hook!

You remind me of one of the emotions; I'm definitely feelin' ya!

I can see the veins in your hand because you definitely caught my eye!

Let's join a fitness club together because I think we will work out!

You're like a kleptomaniac's target; you definitely got what it takes!

I'm gonna change my name to Nick and give you a lifetime basket of food so you can always "pick Nick!"

YO MAMA JOKES

Yo mama is so dumb, she went to a prison to get a cell phone!

Yo mama is so stupid, yo daddy told her they were going to ride in the convertible with the top down, and she came out of the house with no shirt on!

Yo mama is so ugly, she took her kids to the circus and got seven job offers!

Yo mama is so dumb, she went to a Subway restaurant and was mad because the train never showed up!

Yo mama is so skinny, she got a job as a sewing needle!

Yo mama is so dumb, the neighbor asked her if she could borrow a cup of sugar, and yo mama told her to bring the sugar back when she was finished with it!

Yo mama is so dumb, after her boyfriend broke up with her, she bought a Monopoly game so she could have another chance!

Yo mama is so dumb, when she was in line to buy gas and the woman in front of her said, "Fill up on pump nine," yo mama said, "How did you know that guy's name?"

Yo mama is so short, she has to wear shoes on her knees!

Yo mama is so short, she can sit on the curb and swing her legs!

Yo mama is so short, she rode an ant downtown!

Yo mama is so stupid, she put two quarters in her ears and thought she was listening to 50 Cent!

Yo mama is so dumb, she thought a selfie was a service charge for prisoners!

Yo mama is so short, she fell and nobody noticed!

Yo mama is so fat, she jumped in the air and got stuck!

Yo mama's feet are so big, she knocked over five people by crossing her legs!

Yo mama is so ugly, they turned out the lights for Black Friday!

Yo mama is so tall, she walked from Louisville to Lexington in nine steps!

Yo mama is so ugly, she looked in the mirror, and the mirror said, "Hell naw" and called an Uber!

Yo mama is so tall, she got arrested for being a Peeping Tom during airline flights!

Yo mama is so dumb, she dropped an ice cube on the floor then said she hopes he can still rap and act!

Yo mama is so funky, she went swimming in a lake and the fish put in two-week notices!

Yo mama is so skinny, she pooted and broke her back!

Yo mama is so dumb, she wouldn't let her grandson go to sleep because she thought he would be arrested for kidnapping!

Yo mama was so dumb, in elementary school, when the teacher said it was time for recess, yo mama grabbed her hair and said, "No, I like my bangs!"

Yo mama is so ugly, the Grim Reaper filed for unemployment!

Yo mama's hair is so short, you can see what she's thinking from the top of her head!

Yo mama is so skinny, she turned sideways and disappeared!

Yo mama is so dumb, she went to the doctor and when the receptionist said, "Wait here," yo mama said, "One hundred seventy-three pounds, but don't y'all have scales for that?"

Yo mama is so skinny, people hate inviting her to their house because she cuts the furniture!

Yo mama is so dumb, she thought *The Lion King* was a movie about the best fibber!

Yo mama is so fat, she put "Plural" as her relationship status!

Yo mama is so fat, she did twenty sit-ups and didn't move!

Yo mama is so wrinkled, she got a job as a map!

Yo mama is so short, she has to wear ankle socks as leg warmers!

Yo mama is so ugly, the dog brought her the leash to walk her!

Yo mama is so dumb, she went to the Dollar Tree and wanted a price check!

Yo mama is so dumb, she went to a flea market and called them out for false advertising because she didn't see any fleas for sale!

Yo mama is so dumb, when her job told her she'd be working from 5 to 9, she said, "I'm past those ages already, and isn't that too young to work, anyway?"

Yo mama is so dumb, when she was on a plane and the captain said, "Get ready for takeoff," she got mad and dared anyone to touch her clothes!

Yo mama is so ugly, every time she gets in the car, it starts on its own to hurry up the trip!

Yo mama is so dumb, she thought kneecaps were hats for her knees!

Yo mama is so tall, she fell in the street and they thought she was a new bridge!

Yo mama is so stupid, she bought herself a yo-yo and said she could use it to get someone's attention! "Yo, Yo!"

Yo mama is so dumb, she looked at the tag on her shirt, and it said "Made in China," so she called China to see which maid the shirt belonged to!

Yo mama is so stupid, when the mechanic said it was going to cost $80 for the parts and $100 for labor to get her car fixed, she said, "But I'm not pregnant!"

Yo mama is so stupid, a woman beside her started yawning and said, "Ho hum" and yo mama got mad and screamed "Bitch, you hum!"

Yo mama is so dumb, she drove to a left-handers' convention just to see if everyone was alright!

Yo mama is so short, she has to pole vault to get on the curb!

Yo mama is so dumb, the driving instructor told her to hit the brakes and she pulled onto the sidewalk!

Yo mama is so dumb, her friend said she was going to buy some high heels, and yo mama said, "I didn't know you could buy mountains!"

Yo mama is so ugly, she went into a haunted house and came out with a job application!

Yo mama is so fat, she put two cups of water in the tub for bath water, and it still overflowed when she got in!

Yo mama is so stupid, she put paper on top of the TV and called it paper view!

Yo mama is so fat, when she sat at the back of the bus, it did a wheelie!

Yo mama is so dumb, she thought Batman was a baseball player!

Yo mama is so dumb, she thought a Cadillac was feline appreciation!

Yo mama is so dumb, I sent her to the store and told her to bring back change, and she came back with a different dress on!

Yo mama is so dumb, she got a black eye from being poked on Facebook!

Yo mama is so dumb, they asked her to play soccer, and she asked, "What woman do I hit first?"

Yo mama is so tall, she got a window washing job at the Empire State Building!

Yo mama is so dumb, she went to a yard sale and asked the people to help her get the grass home once she made the purchase!

Yo mama is so fat, they wanted to rent her out as an airbag for buses!

Yo mama is so fat, she took one step and had to wait fifteen minutes for the rest of her to catch up!

Yo mama is so stupid, when they told her to catch the bus, she ran back in the house to get her softball glove!

Yo mama is so dumb, she bought an Echo and thought she should get a new car every minute!

Yo mama is so dumb, she went to the Army, and when they said "Attack!" she screamed out, "A paperclip!"

Yo mama is so stupid, she climbed over a see-through glass wall to see what was on the other side!

Yo mama is so dumb, yo daddy told her to let the dog out, and she said, "Woof, woof woof!"

Yo mama is so dumb, she thought a microwave was a midget saying goodbye!

Yo mama is so stupid, she went to Walmart and asked the salesperson, "How much are your walls?"

Yo mama is so fat, when she turns around, people throw her a welcome back party!

Yo mama is so stupid, she tried to put M&Ms in alphabetical order!

Yo mama is so fat, I took a picture of her last Christmas, and it's still printing!

Yo mama is so stupid, when your dad said, "It's chilly outside," she ran out the door with a spoon, bowl, and crackers!

Yo mama is so fat, the last time she saw 90210 was on a scale!

Yo mama is so dumb, yo daddy told her to turn the TV on, so she started stripping in front of the flat screen!

THE REST OF YO FAMILY JOKES

Yo Daddy

Yo daddy is so short, he stood up and was the same height.

Yo daddy is so short, he can play kickball with roaches!

Yo daddy is so dumb, somebody told him to call an ambulance, and he said, "What should I call it?"

Yo daddy is so dumb, his lawyer told him he needed a will, and he said, "I got four of 'em on my car, five if you count the spare. Can I use one of them?"

Yo daddy is so dumb, the eye doctor asked him if he's ever had cataracts, and he said, "No, never even drove one. I have had three Oldsmobiles, though!"

Yo daddy is so dumb, a guy told him it was seventy-five degrees outside, and yo daddy said, "Come on, I'll help you pick them up; they must have blown away from a graduation nearby!"

Yo daddy is so short, he tripped on a raisin!

Yo daddy is so short, he sneezed and killed an ant colony!

Yo daddy is so dumb, the doctor told him he should get his colon checked, and he said, "Why? It still has a good scent to it, especially the spray!"

Yo daddy is so fat, he got a job as shade!

Yo daddy is so dumb, he went to a yard sale and asked the homeowner, "How much are you selling your grass for?"

Yo daddy is so dumb, he got beat up because he dented the hood of someone's car after they asked if he could give it a jump.

Yo daddy is so stupid, he was in church, and the pastor said, "Let the church say amen." Yo stupid daddy said, "There's women in here too, Pastor!"

Yo daddy is so dumb, when he was watching a football game and a team got a fifteen-yard penalty, he said, "Damn, they got a lot of grass to cut after the game!"

Yo daddy is so slow, turtles are going on strike!

Yo daddy is so short, he can change your oil without a jack!

Yo daddy is so fat, he has to use roll-on deodorant!

Yo daddy is so short, he has to stand on his tiptoes to see over the curb!

Yo daddy is so dumb, he went to his bank, and the teller said he had ten withdrawals last month, and he said, "But I don't even smoke!"

Yo daddy is so short, he put on a hat and immediately thought it was nighttime!

Yo daddy is so short, he can limbo under an ant!

Yo daddy is so stupid, he took a trip to the coroner's laboratory, saw a skeleton on a steel table, and said, "Look, a slab of ribs!"

Yo daddy is so short, his arms look like crutches!

Yo daddy is so short, he had to use a ladder to take his next step!

Yo daddy is so dumb, he thought Piggly Wiggly was a strip club for hogs!

Yo daddy is so dumb, yo mama told him to let the dog out, so he went to try and pimp some women!

Yo daddy is so dumb, he only listens to rap music at Christmastime!

Yo daddy is so tall, he fell and his head was in the next state!

Yo daddy is so dumb, he went to IHOP and started jumping on one leg!

Yo daddy is so dumb, he got stuck in a revolving door!

Yo daddy is so dumb, he thought a liquor store was a brothel!

Yo daddy's hands are so small, they nicknamed him Microwave!

Yo daddy is so short, he tried to run and got tackled by an ant!

Yo daddy is so dumb, he thought a fishing license was for fish that drove!

Yo daddy is so skinny, he got a job posing for stick figures!

Yo daddy is so dumb, they told him to go through the drive-through window, so he got out of his car and climbed inside the restaurant!

Yo daddy is so stupid, he thought a mammogram was a woman buying cocaine!

Yo daddy is so stupid, he got pulled over for speeding, and the officer said, "Do you know how fast you were going?" and yo daddy said, "Faster than you for about three miles!"

Yo daddy is so dumb, someone told him to take a shower and he got caught shoplifting at Home Depot!

Yo daddy's nose is so big, he sneezed and blew off four people's clothes in front of him!

Yo daddy is so dumb, he's been sitting at the stop sign for three days waiting for it to say "Go!"

Yo daddy is so ugly, he had to tie a dog around his neck to eat a pork chop!

Yo daddy and his twin are so skinny, they rent themselves out as knitting needles!

Yo daddy is so short, he walks around high fiving ants!

Yo daddy is so stupid, a small group asked him to take a picture of them, and he said "Where is it? And why do you want me to have it? 'Cause I don't know y'all!"

Yo daddy's head is so skinny, it looks like a butterfly!

Yo daddy is so dumb, you asked him to go to the drive-through window of a restaurant, and he said, "OK, but I don't see how this car is gonna fit through the little opening!"

Yo daddy is so fat, he took a deep breath and sucked up three dogs, a tree, and a minivan!

Yo daddy is so dumb, he thought he was gonna get arrested for money laundering after he took his jeans out of the dryer and found three quarters in his pocket!

Yo daddy is so pigeon-toed and bow-legged, he can spell "OX" all by himself!

Yo daddy is so short, he walked in a puddle and had to dog-paddle out!

Yo daddy is so tall, he got a job swatting birds off telephone lines!

Yo daddy is so stupid, he thought the Goodwill store was a place that never sold bad wheels!

Yo daddy is so short, he rides ants for fun!

Yo daddy is so dumb, yo mama told him to run her some bath water, so he got a bucket, filled it up in the tub, then sprinted outside!

Yo daddy is so short, he stuck his tongue out and tripped!

Yo daddy is so tall, he tripped on a rock and fell for ten minutes!

Yo daddy is so skinny, he rents himself out as a baton to high school majorettes!

Yo daddy's head is so big, he can't stop nodding!

Yo daddy is so stupid, he thought Fox News was a women's magazine!

Yo daddy is so fat, he fell five times and didn't know it!

Yo daddy's head is so big, they use him as a human compass!

Yo daddy is so dumb, he thought "doggy style" was a fashion magazine for canines!

Yo daddy is so fat, he went on a cruise and had to get off the ship to help push it from the dock, then he jumped back on!

Yo daddy is so dumb, he thought a V6 was an off-brand tomato drink!

Yo daddy is so dumb, his friends asked him if he wanted to pick up some girls, and he said, "I will if they aren't too heavy!"

Yo daddy is so dumb, when they told him he was selected for jury duty, he said, "Hell naw, let them clean their own bathrooms!"

Yo daddy is so dumb, he thought he could make a living by thinking because somebody told him, "A penny for your thoughts," and he had over one thousand thoughts a day.

Yo daddy was so dumb in high school, when they voted him homecoming king, he went home!

Yo daddy's head is so big, he leaned forward and now he's a permanent break dancer!

Yo daddy is so skinny, he got a job at Kroger as a meat slicer!

Yo daddy is so dumb, his friend asked him to call him a cab, and he said, "But isn't your name Steve?"

Yo daddy is so dumb, somebody asked him if he could give them a jump, and he said, "How high?"

Yo daddy is so short, he needs an elevator to get on the curb!

Yo daddy is so dumb, he thought a pork chop was a pig doing karate!

Yo daddy is so dumb, his boss told him to take a break, so he went outside, jacked somebody's car up, and took a wheel off!

Yo daddy is so dumb, they told him to go deer hunting, and he came home with three Swedish models!

Yo daddy is so dumb, he thought "Puff, puff, pass" was P Diddy taking instructions as a quarterback from the sideline coach!

Yo daddy is so dumb, somebody told him his fly was open, and he said, "I just swatted 'em. I don't remember cutting 'em!"

Yo daddy's neck is so long, he took y'all to the zoo and when y'all got to the giraffe section, one of the giraffes looked over at yo daddy and said, "Cousin, what's up?"

Yo daddy is so stupid, he thought a three-piece suit was clothing you wear to KFC!

Yo Little Brother

Yo little brother is so stupid, the teacher told him they were going to have a multiple choice test tomorrow, and he said, "Cool, my choice is not to take it!"

Yo little brother is so short, they hired him as a hood emblem!

Yo little brother is so dumb, he went to get an oil change and told them to put in something different!

Yo little brother's arms are so short, he has to dress up as a T.rex every Halloween!

Yo little brother's head is so big, his neck has to take steroids!

Yo little brother's arms are so long, he got a job stopping traffic for trains at a railroad crossing!

Yo little brother's head is so big, it looks like his neck is blowing a bubble!

Yo little brother is so dumb, he has to wear a helmet to think!

Yo little brother's head is so big, he has to run everywhere he goes!

Yo Granddaddy

Yo granddaddy is so old, he sneezed and lost two toes!

Yo granddaddy is so old, he was before the chicken *and* the egg!

Yo granddaddy is so old, he made the hill *then* went over it!

Yo granddaddy is so old, he poots air from 1910!

Yo granddaddy is so old, his kidneys have gray hair!

Yo granddaddy is so old, his first watch was a sundial!

Yo granddaddy is so old, he still has the scar on his head from the camel that kicked him on the Ark!

Yo granddaddy is so old, his birth year is three digits!

Yo granddaddy is so old, he took an hour nap and woke up with a five-foot beard!

Yo granddaddy is so old, he still has cans of Dinosaur Chow in his cabinet!

Yo granddaddy is so stupid, he waited for a sign that said "Gas next exit" so he could fart!

Yo granddaddy is so old, he got an autograph from Moses!

Yo granddaddy is so old, somebody asked him, "What's your sign?" and he said, "One if by land, two if by sea!"

Yo granddaddy is so old, they told him they were going to take the train to New York, and he asked where Harriet Tubman was!

Yo Sister

Yo sister is so dumb, the teacher told her they were going to have a spelling bee at school tomorrow, and she said, "I didn't know bees could talk!"

Yo sister is so dumb, when yo mama said she was going to whoop her ass, she started laughing because she knew y'all didn't own a donkey. Then you laughed because you pictured yo mama whooping a donkey!

Yo sister is so dumb, she went to Kmart to find the other twenty-five letters!

Yo sister is so short, she plays hopscotch on her hands!

Yo sister is so fat, she's always on a roll!

Yo sister is so stupid, she thought a haircut was a weave discount!

Yo sister is so skinny, she rents herself out to restaurants as a toothpick!

Yo sister is so stupid, somebody told her to get a life and she went out and bought the board game!

Yo sister is so tall, she hurdles city buses in traffic!

Yo sister is so ugly, she has to tie a dog around her neck so a bone will play with her!

Yo sister is so skinny, she gave her friend a high five and cut off three of her fingers!

Yo sister is so tall, she got arrested for sniffing clouds!

Yo sister is so skinny, she got a job as a speedometer needle!

Yo sister is so skinny, she swallowed a grape and they thought she was eight months pregnant!

Yo sister is so ugly, she fell face down and the sidewalk pushed her back up!

Yo sister is so skinny, she can be the ring toss pole while playing with Cheerios!

Yo sister is so dumb, yo mama told her to walk the dog, so she climbed on the dog's back!

Yo sister's hands are so small, they hired her to perform surgery on flies!

Yo sister is so tall, she does roofing without a ladder!

Yo sister is so tall, she got a job as a window washer for a ten-story building without a ladder!

Yo sister's butt is so flat, she has to attach four chair legs to it to sit down!

Yo sister's teeth are so yellow, she got a job dipping them in water to make lemonade!

Yo sister's so dumb, she went to Walmart to see if Trump was still going to have one built!

Yo sister's hair is so nappy, she got a part-time job scrubbing barbeque grills!

Yo sister's hair is so nappy, Madam CJ Walker came back to life just to make her some new products!

Yo Cousin

Yo cousin is so stupid, when he was working at the Burger King drive-through, he asked the driver what his order was, and when the driver said, "Whopper with cheese," he smacked a female coworker in the head with a slice of cheese!

Yo cousin is so stupid, he was happy the teacher said they were going to have a pop quiz because his daddy worked at Pepsi!

Yo cousin is so skinny, he got a job slim-jimming cars!

Yo cousin is so stupid, he went to a brothel to get ho-made food!

Yo cousin's baby mama is so stupid, when the doctor said he makes house calls, she said, "Does it answer?"

Yo cousin's jaws are so saggy, it looks like his nose is lifting weights!

Yo Uncle

Yo uncle is so dumb, somebody told him he should run for president, and he said, "Can't I walk?"

Yo uncle is so short, he can kick his own ass!

Yo uncle is so dumb, he thought a police escort was a souped-up Ford hatchback with a siren!

Yo uncle is so dumb, he went to a garage sale and asked the homeowner, "Where are you going to park your cars after you sell your garage, and will you deliver it if I buy it?"

Yo uncle is so dumb, he asked a couple where they were going, and when they said, "Movies," yo dumb uncle said, "Move what, and where do you want them moved to?"

Yo uncle is so stupid, when somebody asked him to help them pick some greens, he said, "Hunter, lime, mint, sage."

Yo uncle is so dumb, when his car was almost out of gas and he saw a sign that said "Gas 5 miles," he kept driving because he wanted to get a lot more than five miles when he filled up!

Yo uncle is so dumb, he thought a forest fire was Gump losing his job!

Yo uncle is so short, he got arrested for robbing a roach motel!

Yo uncle is so skinny, somebody gave him a pat on the back and missed!

Yo uncle is so stupid, when the car salesman asked if he wanted to take a test drive, yo uncle said, "Is it gonna be true or false or multiple choice?"

Yo uncle is so short, he has to tiptoe to see over the curb!

Yo uncle is so tall, he has to duck for planes!

Yo uncle is so stupid, he went to a baseball game for the first time and when the umpire said "Strike three!" yo dumbass uncle hit two people and was going after the third one before security tackled him!

Yo uncle is so dumb, he thought the dry cleaner closed when it rained!

Yo uncle is so short, he got jumped by three people and they missed him!

Yo uncle is so stupid, he went to the Dollar Tree to see if they needed their leaves raked!

Yo uncle is so dumb, he called the transportation department and wanted them to remove a "Deer Crossing" sign because he waited for two hours and never saw any!

Yo uncle is so dumb, a friend of his told him his son was in the Armed Forces, and yo dumb uncle said, "Duh, you can't shoot a gun without arms!"

Yo uncle is so dumb, when someone asked him if he knew what time it was, he said, "Yep!"

Yo Auntie

Yo auntie is so dumb, when your uncle told her he passed gas, she said, "Don't you have a full tank anyway?"

Yo auntie's ears are so big, the neighborhood connected cable to them and got 115 channels!

Yo auntie is so stupid, she put a calendar on her front porch so she could go out on a date!

Yo auntie is so short, she has toes on her knees!

Yo auntie is so tall, she got a job passing out peanuts on flights from the ground!

Yo auntie is so dumb, she wore a bikini in a carpool!

Yo auntie is so stupid, her friend told her she was feeling sleepy, and yo auntie replied, "Leave that dwarf alone; aren't you married?"

Yo auntie is so stupid, her friend told her she was taking her to a steakhouse for dinner, and yo stupid auntie said, "I didn't know they built houses out of meat!"

Yo auntie is so skinny, she bought herself some knitting needles, and she could've sworn one of them said, "Wassup, fam?"

Yo auntie's breath is so bad, she got a winter job lighting fireplaces!

Yo auntie is so dumb, she thought the Bee Gees were insect playas!

Yo auntie is so tall, she has to put a light on the top of her head for the planes!

Yo auntie is so dumb, she saw a man pulling a cow across the street and said, "Look, Hamburger Helper!"

Yo auntie is so skinny, she put two marbles in her back pockets so she could have a butt!

Yo auntie is so fat, the airbags in her car asked to be removed because they didn't like the competition!

Yo auntie's fingernails are so long, she got a job as a back scratcher in the next county—and she works from home!

Yo auntie is so tall, she got a job brushing snow off of mountaintops!

Yo auntie is so dumb, she angrily went to Popeyes looking for Olive Oyl and when she couldn't find her, she said, "She must be chicken!"

Yo auntie is so skinny, she pushed her way through a crowd and cut fifteen people!

Yo auntie is so ugly, she looked in the mirror and her reflection busted out laughing!

Yo auntie is so dumb, somebody told her they were going to take a road trip, and she said, "Don't fall too hard; that asphalt is hard!"

Yo Granny

Yo granny is so old, she coughed up dust from World War I!

Yo granny is so stupid, when the doctor told her she had pneumonia, she said, "No, I didn't have to buy any this time; I still have some old ammonia left from my last grocery store visit!"

Yo granny is so old, her teeth have teeth!

Yo granny is so short, she got mugged by a cricket!

Yo granny is so fat, she jumped in the air and stopped time!

Yo granny is so old, she used to beat up Moses at recess!

Yo granny is so old, she used to babysit Moses!

Yo granny is so old, she has tea in her cabinet from the Boston Tea Party!

Yo granny is so dumb, she went to the post office looking for fence support material!

Yo granny is so short, she entered the rodeo riding a squirrel!

Yo granny is so old, she has whiskers on her whiskers!

Yo granny is so old, she still has scars on her feet from being the brakes on a covered wagon!

Yo granny is so short, she can ride a Chihuahua!

Yo granny is so short, she got a pat on the back from a cricket!

Yo granny is so old, she took a picture with Lazarus!

Yo granny is so old, she tried to rap hieroglyphics!

Yo granny is so old, she still has Harriet Tubman's number on speed dial!

Yo granny is so skinny, the wind tapped her on the shoulder to see if she was really there!

Yo granny is so short, she has to get a running start to jump to conclusions!

Yo granny is so old, she still has steam burns from the first locomotive!

Yo granny is so old, she still has pork ribs in her freezer from Noah's Ark!

Yo granny is so old, she still has the first place trophy from the Miss Garden of Eden pageant!

Yo granny is so old, she served dessert at the last supper!

Yo granny is so dumb, she thought Krispy Kreme was a stripper's stage name!

Yo granny is so old, she still has the scarf Harriet Tubman gave her for Christmas!

Yo granny is so wrinkled, she got a job as a prune spokesperson!

Yo granny is so old, her wrinkle's wrinkles have wrinkles!

Yo granny is so old, her first address was 1 Garden of Eden Avenue!

Yo granny is so old, she's not over the hill, she's over the mountain!

Yo granny is so short, she has to put on high heels to stand up!

Yo granny is so old, she still has her passport from the Ark.

Yo granny is so old, she still has a Flintstones phone!

Yo granny's teeth are so big, she's got a permanent smile!

Yo granny is so old, she's started growing baby teeth all over again!

Yo granny's legs are so hairy, somebody asked if her acupuncture hurt!

Yo granny is so wrinkled, they said she was "raisin" hell!

Yo granny's eyes are so big, she can see your future!

Yo granny's tongue is so long, she got recruited to be a "no hands" pickpocket!

Yo granny is so old, when someone asked if she wanted anything from White Castle, she said, "Yes, but be careful crossing the moat!"

Yo granny is so dumb, when she got arrested and was told she needed to get her mug shot taken, she said, "I don't drink, and shouldn't it be a shot glass, anyway?"

MISCELLANEOUS JOKES

What do country people drink out of? / Hiccups!

I went to the dentist for a cleaning. In the next room, a dental assistant was right beside the dentist when something from the patient's mouth landed in her hand. The dentist said, "Are you in here catching 'fillings' for me?"

I was in Kroger, and I saw a lady's wig fall into the shopping cart! I said, "Look, basket weave!"

A bakery company was on strike, and their signs read, "No Loafing, Got No Bread!"

I was at a Christian book store when I saw this cute old couple. They were getting ready to leave, and the wife said to the husband, "Dear, get my cane if you're able!"

I went to get some poster paper, and the cashier said, "That's $2.99 plus fifteen cents for the tax!" I said, "Don't worry about the tacks; we can't put holes in the wall, so we will use tape!"

One friend asked another friend if he knew somebody who could build a boat. The other friend said, "Yes, I Noah man!"

I was in a doctor's office with many other people when a nurse came through the door and screamed, "Bend over!" Everyone in the room bent down, but one man stood up and said, "Get up, fools. My name is Ben Dover!"

One guy was asked what it was like to work for the Planters company, and he said he worked with a bunch of nuts!

A woman returned defective candles because they just didn't make scents!

A man who lived up many stairs ordered a pizza. The delivery guy was walking up the steps and the man heard him and waited in the doorway. The delivery driver tripped on the last step and the pizza went flying, landing all over the man in the door. The man got really mad and was ready to fight when he told the delivery driver, "Come on, you wanna pizza me?"

What did the female fitness center employee say to the male fitness center employee who wanted to date her? / "I'm sorry; I just don't think we will work out!"

A man walked into a bar. He wasn't hurt seriously, though.

Amtrak trains are soliciting businesses on their late-night train service. The first business that opened on the train was a hair salon; they were weaving on that midnight train to Georgia!

Walgreens: the result of a food fight with kale, mustards, and collards!

A cigarette walked into a bar, but it got put out!

If you have a weave made out of horse hair, how do you "mane-tain" it?

Someone asked me if they could borrow a couple of bucks. I said, "Sorry, I don't have the doe!"

I went to Wendy's and was blown away.

I was in Subway the other day and a guy walked in and asked me if I knew what time the next train arrived.

I went to the doctor to get a shot; they have some good bourbon!

A friend of mine wanted me to meet the new librarian. I said, "I'll go check her out!"

I went to a camera shop to see what was clickin'!

Anybody want crab legs? I do, but I'd walk funny!

I went to a kangaroo party, and the place was jumping!

I went to the store to get some bread, but I was short on dough.

I went up to a bare tree to see if there was anything I could do. The tree said, "Just leave me!"

A stripper went to a full-service gas station, and the attendant came out and said, "Feel 'er up?"

Jiffy Lube: another term for greasing your cornbread pan!

Someone said to me, "Can I ask you a question?" I said, "Didn't you just ask me a question?"

Someone knocked a sex pill on the floor. I said, "Viagra falls!"

If a bird gets slapped, does he turn the other beak?

Illegal drug maker's advice: Don't "meth" with him!

If you have a brain fart, shouldn't steam come out of your ears?

I went to a carpet store and the salesman kept trying to get me to buy some carpet! I called him a "rug pusher!"

When someone says, "I'm gonna lose it," are they letting you know so you can help them find it?

A plumbers favorite song: "Back That Thang Up"

A bucket list: 1) Bucket

If someone calls you a cab, what would you call them?

Someone was wondering who owned the rights to the *60 Minutes* TV show. The owners came forward and said, "It's 'hour' show!"

A minute should be fat because it always has sixty seconds!

If someone tells you to "put a little spring in your step," would you plant flowers in your shoes?

If a horse moved next door to you, it would be your new nayyybor!

I saw a baby smile really big after crying, and I said, "Look, whine and cheese!"

Do you need a sturdy boat built? I Noah man!

If you drive a Rolls Royce to a restaurant in the evening, could that be called "Dinner Rolls?"

Do you think the workers at Rolex, Seiko, and Timex are watched?

Why do they call them doughnut holes? You cannot eat a hole! Why not call them doughnut cutouts?

Never name a rabbit "Celie!"

If you've ever lost your mind ... I forgot what I was about to say.

A pilot always "takes off" from work!

If a mailman drops a letter, will he stamp on it?

Always duck a goose! Never goose a duck!

Never shoot craps with a person who has diarrhea!

Never answer a call from a postman on the third ring!

Never say "Take it from me" to a robber!

Did "Paul Bear" Bryant always have to go to funerals to assist with the casket?

Never buy a female serial killer a choker necklace!

Never tell a vacuum cleaner salesman that his product sucks!

Never tell a teacher they have no class!

Never, ever say "Well, I'll be a monkey's uncle!" to your nephew or niece.

Never give tulips to someone who loves to talk!

Never tell a cop to "give it a rest!"

Never tell a puppeteer to "talk to the hand!"

Never think a cab driver is "fare" game!

Never tell an elevator operator your ups and downs!

Never tell a brain surgeon to "mind his own business!"

Never tell a stripper to "grin and bare it!"

A true horse rider will saddle for anything!

Never tell a pickle maker "dill with it."

Never say "You just can't beat it!" to a drum player.

Do piano players ever lose their keys?

Never "pick" with a guitar player!

Never ask a clock maker "What time is it?"

Never tell a tow truck driver "Let's hook up!"

Never say "That's alright" to a left-handed person!

Never say "You're a little touched!" to a person who just got a massage.

Never say "Oh, rats" in a Chinese restaurant!

Never ask a happy person "Are you Pharrell?"

Never, ever tell a pyromaniac "Let's burn one!"

Never ask a high person "What's the buzz?"

Never tell a midget "I don't get down like that!"

Never tell a skinny person "Break a leg!"

Never tell an ox a bad "yoke!"

Never tell a makeup artist "Get outta my face!"

Never sit a stinky person in a church "pew!"

Never tell a deranged person with scissors to "cut it out!"

Never tell a dentist "You know the drill!"

Never watch Snow White and say, "I'm sleepy!"

Never ask a podiatrist to foot the bill!

Never tell a midget they are a little short on cash!

Never say "What's up?" to a guy with sagging pants!

Never say "I can dig it" when you're at a funeral!

Never say "I'm about to turn up" when picking greens!

When you apologize to a woman for being sexually flirty, never say "My bad!"

Never ask an Eskimo "Are you chillin?"

Never say hi to your friend Jack on an airplane. "Hi, Jack!"

Never tell a dog catcher "It's rough out here!"

Never ask a gynecologist "You feel me?"

Never tell a pyromaniac "You're fired!"

Never tell a dyslexic person to "pee and go to bed!"

I had a woman get mad at me because I bought her a box of diapers after she told me she wanted to be pampered!

Woman: "I can't keep a man."
Friend: "It could be your name."
Woman: "Really? How?"
Friend: "What's your name?"
Woman: "It's Aleva Malone!"

Cop: "Do you know how fast you were going?"
Driver: "Faster than you for a little while!"

Cop: "Do you know why I pulled you over?"
Driver: "Well, you really didn't pull me over. I slowed down and carefully steered off the road!"

Why do I feel like a Snickers bar is always laughing at me?

You ever run out of money so fast that a C note turned into a "saw" note?

Why do most singers sing "Naw, naw, naw, naw" in their song? Do they not believe the verse they just sang?

Traffic school is for drivers with no class!

Being called a stand-up guy didn't sit too well with him!

If you have a cow for a pet, can you be charged for "pettin'" leather?

People named William have to have all the money; everyone pays Bills!

Someone asked me what "poke" meant. I said, "It's meat from a pig!"

I went to Kmart but got put out because I bought the letter M!

Someone said, "The joke's on you," and I'm still looking for writing on my clothes!

Someone asked me if I had change for a five, and I said, "Six!"

A guy asked me if I had any spare change. I said, "Nope, none of my other four tires have gone flat yet!"

I said I wanted doughnuts, and someone pointed at some rich idiots!

The entire alphabet went on a field trip and almost forgot the P. They held the bus for him, and when he got on, one of the letters said, "Since you're late, 'urine' the back of the bus!"

A cop pulled me over and told me I was under arrest. I said, "Thanks, but how did you know I was tired?"

I tried to dot my I's and cross my T's, and I wound up almost blind and spilling two cups of my favorite drink!

Someone: "What's up?"
Me: "Everyone except the people who are asleep!"

I went to an amusement park, and I was very amused at people's parking!

Years ago, I tried to have a relationship with a ghost, but there just wasn't anything there!

I hate when you go through the drive-through and the person says, "Can I take your order?" No, I just wanted to see if this big, bright sign could really talk!

When you are at a store and the clearance sale sign says, "50% off," and another sticker on the signs says, "Take an additional 50% off clearance items," shouldn't you get those items for free?

I went to a popular restaurant to eat late-night breakfast, and I started to get dizzy and my legs almost gave out on me. I got weak in "Denny's!"

A coach had a watch clipped to his belt. That was a waist of time!

The doctor told a woman she was retaining water, and she said, "Well, I'll be dam!"

I went to McDonald's, and the French fries were really good. The manager came out and said, "Because it's Good Fry Day!"

I went to the doctor, and she said I have acute bursitis. I said, "Thanks for the compliment; I try!"

A man was caught cooking drugs in his house. He methed up!

Someone said thirty feet is equal to ten yards. After measuring to the tenth house on my street, I realized they need to go back to math school!

I went to Burger King and asked the manager if I could still have it my way. The manager said, "Yes," so I said, "I want this building torn down and rebuilt seventy-five feet longer!"

Someone: "You went out on a limb for that one."
Me: "Yeah, I'm just 'branching' out. 'Leave' me alone, or I will go to my 'trunk'!"

One of the schools I went to wasn't exciting. I was a black bored!

Someone asked me if I was going to ride with the top down today. I said, "No, I dress decent!"

A guy told me that he likes to pull the skin off of rabbits and minks. I said, "What fur?"

Someone: "Hey, look, the sun is out!"
Me: "Uh, no it isn't; it's still burning!"

Somebody was bragging and said, "I got three degrees!" I said, "That's pretty cool!"

I lost my watch, and my mama put me in time out!

I got mud and grass stains on my pants as a kid, and my mama said I was grounded!

Someone: "I broke wind."
Me: "No, you produced wind."
Someone: "Makes scents to me!"

I went to the ear doctor, and he said, "Come hear!"

Who says strippers don't have jobs; they go "t-werk" every day!

Someone said, "Run that by me again," so I backed up about thirty feet then ran toward them while repeating what I said!

I went to JCPenney, and I didn't spend a dime!

I went to Dunkin' Donuts the other day. I think I'll switch back to a basketball, though—less mess and no food waste!

I went to the eye doctor, and he put me in the I-C-U!

I just heard that some cops are overworked. Aw, "po-po" thangs!

Lady 1: "Do you have a bun in the oven?"
Lady 2: "No, I turn my stove off before I leave the house!"

I saw a midget trying to flag me down for something, and I said, "Look, a microwave!"

I was learning how to make yeast rolls, and the instructor said, "First, I knead my dough!" I said, "Don't worry, I'm gonna pay you as soon as the class is over!"

Stores lie when they say their doors are open twenty-four hours. Every time I go, I have to push or pull to get inside!

Little Bo Peep, so the lady across the street closed her curtains!

Someone asked me what time I went to sleep. I said, "I don't know; I wasn't awake at the time!"

Someone: "Congratulations, you made the honor roll."
Me: "I didn't think my joke was *that* funny in the courtroom!"

A yellow jacket landed on my arm but didn't sting me. I said, "Well, that's a humble bee!"

I saw a girl throw Valentine's candy at her boyfriend; she gave him a heart attack!

I went to an abandoned air freshener factory. That didn't make no scents at all!

They say quarter horses have more cents.

Some cows went on strike, so the farmer called a meeting. When they all got there, the farmer said, "So, what's your beef? Y'all already milking the clock!" The cows said, "We just want 'stable' employment like the horses, mane!"

I went to Arby's and ordered some "curly" fries, and the cashier said, "Larry the cook said we don't have no Moe!"

A guy bought a seeing eye dog and started to crank his tail. I asked him what was he doing, and he said, "Focusing!"

I went to a steakhouse, and when the waitress served my plate, my T-bone flew off the plate and on the floor. I tried to catch it, but that was a big "missed steak!"

I stepped on a bug. I guess I shoe-d him!

A flat-chested lady applied to Hooters because she needed a boob job!

I lost my voice because I was hoarsing around!

Someone told me the answer was as clear as glass. I cracked up!

A doctor told a woman she needed more iron. She was steamed!

Someone asked me if I had change for a dollar, and I said, "Sure" and put on a different outfit—*and* took the dollar!

One bag of weed said to the other bag of weed, "Can I be blunt with ya?"

I've been given one minute to eat. I won't starve after the first helping because I'll have sixty seconds.

Art got arrested. He said he was framed!

Rudolph was spotted in a strip club shouting, "Make it rain, dear!"

A skeleton was trying to fight me, but I told him he didn't have the guts!

Someone told me they wanted some crab legs, and I said, "You'd walk awful funny!"

A salesman asked me if he could have a minute of my time. I said, "No, I need all my minutes; get your own!"

A chiropractor's slogan: "Let's get it back-a-crackin!"

One egg said to the other egg, "Man, you had me cracking up at your yolks when we were sitting on your poach!"

I used to play with scissors, but I cut that out!

I sprayed some Raid and a little bitty swat team invaded my house and arrested me!

I know a lady so skinny that she used to work as a sewing needle threader!

I would say a molehill is a mountain to an ant.

I know a guy that's so tall, he can smell the peanuts on airplanes!

I used to think a popsicle was your daddy riding a bike!

Man: "Is it cold enough for ya?"
Me: "No, I want it to be cryogenics level!"

A podiatrist is always concerned about who will foot the bill!

A foot surgeon's favorite words after reattaching toes to feet: "Toed ya!"

I got suspended from school once. The fire department finally came and got me down!

I was at a pool hall, and one guy told the other, "I'm a pool 'shark' because I'm 'fin' to whoop you in eight-ball!"

I stopped going to garage sales. The guy at the last one wouldn't sell the garage. False advertising!

Why call it a two-car garage with one car parked in it? Just call it a one-car garage with potential!

Someone asked me if I could write in cursive, and I said, "Sure, $&@#%*+?!$&@."

I went to a yard sale, left one hundred dollars with the lady, and rented a sod cutter!

My steering wheel broke one day, and I could only turn left. That just wasn't right!

I went to the shoe store to get a certain pair of shoes. They ran out!

What do women wear in Barcelona? / Spain-dex!

I saw an alligator smoking weed, I said, "Croc-pot!"

I saw a mama bumblebee disciplining her kids. She said, "Hey, kids, you better beehive yourselves!"

A guy let some of his friends snort some cocaine through a rolled-up five dollar bill. I said, "Look, he gave everybody a high five!"

I went bowling for the first time with some friends, and when I bowled, I didn't knock all the pins down. One guy told me I could pick up a spare, so I went to my car, opened my trunk, and said, "This is a weird game!"

The warden took some prisoners fishing, and they used jailbait!

Someone asked me if I could burn a CD for them, and I said, "Sure, you got a lighter?"

One guy asked another guy if he prayed. The other guy said, "Yes, but I try not to be too obvious to my victims!"

Man: "I heard you graduated!"
Student: "Yes, sir, cum laude."
Man: "Oh, and you sing gospels, too, huh?"

Do bees have honey-do lists?

I saw a gang of dogs riding motorcycles. They called themselves the Ruff Riders!

A car said to a motorcycle, "Dude, when are we going to roll?" The motorcycle said, "No time soon; I'm two-tired!"

I saw a cow with no legs, and I said, "Look, ground beef!"

If you don't discipline your cows, would you get spoiled milk?

I flipped my iPhone on the other side, and someone asked me what was I doing. I said, "I am making an apple turnover!"

Bartender: "Can someone call this man a cab?" The whole bar: "Hey, Cab!"

If horses move next door to you, would you help them saddle in?

If someone steals your pig, is that called a ham hock?

I went to the door store; they were closed!

A friend of mine wanted to borrow five bucks. I said, "It's not deer season yet, so you're short on doe, huh?"

I found three dollars in my jeans pocket after they had been washed. I got arrested for money laundering!

Farmer 1: "What are you growing this year?"
Farmer 2: "Corn."
Farmer 1: "It's gonna be on and poppin' later, huh?"

A driver pulled up to another driver who had a flat tire and asked him, "Do you have a spare?" The driver with the flat said, "Yes, but I need it for my own car!" That is a tired joke!

One shoe said to the other shoe, "Hey, you're my sole mate!"

I threw my calendar away because it was dated!

Someone asked me if I wanted to get into a carpool. I said, "How does the water stay in?"

Woman: "Are they twins?"
Me: "Only when they're together!"

A lady stopped another lady who had two little boys with the same hairstyle, same outfit, and were the same height. She asked the lady, "Are they twins?" The lady sarcastically said, "No, it's only one boy holding a mirror!"

Someone told me it was seventy degrees outside, and I said, "I'll help you pick them up; they must've blown away from a college graduation!"

I saw a person who was so dumb trying to get a buy one, get one free deal. He asked the cashier how much the second item was, and the cashier said, "No charge," so he pulled out his checkbook, and said, "Well, do you take checks?"

I went to the store and asked the cashier if everything was a dollar? She said, "Yes," so I left $1.06 on the counter and took a shopping cart!

I had a hard time parallel parking. I couldn't get anyone to pull up next to me and do exactly what I did!

I went to a gas station and saw my friend "Phillip" on pump 7!

I went to Target to get some practice!

I went to Sears thinking it was the eye doctor!

I stood in line at Subway and never saw or heard a train come through!

If money doesn't grow on trees, where did all of these Dollar Trees come from?

Somebody told me I was on a roll, but I didn't get good grades in school!

I went to five different Dollar Stores and not one of them sold any dollars!

What are y'all doing at soccer practice? Aw, we just "kickin' it!"

What do I do when I see the prices at Ben & Jerry's? "I scream!"

I saw a customer "clowning" at Shoe Carnival!

Someone told me they wanted to be a child again, and I said, "You've got to be kidding!"

I went to buy some diapers, and the salesperson said it was $7.99 for the diapers and $0.48 cents for the tax. I said, "We use safety pins, not tacks!"

I went to the chiropractor and left my license at the office. I went "straight back!"

I went to the dentist because I couldn't handle the tooth!

A girl was dancing while driving to her job and when somebody asked her where she was going, she said, "T-werk!"

I went to the store and paid for one item, then had to go back in and buy something else. I used two separate checks. The cashier said, "Discount double check!"

I wanted to stick my arm in a fan, but somebody said it wasn't worth the wrist!

The front of my shoes were pointed upward, and somebody said, "I was 'toe' up!"

My leg was itching, so I scratched it, and somebody said I nailed it!

I wanted to clip coupons, but somebody said, "Cut it out."

Somebody laughed because I sneezed. I told them it was "snot" funny!

Somebody told me they felt sleepy, so I called them a pervert and told them to leave the other six dwarfs alone!

I told someone I loved fall weather, and they said, "Quit tripping!"

I was mad because of a bad pedicure. Somebody said, "You don't take de-feet very well!"

I was going to quit driving, and somebody said, "Yes, you need a brake!"

I was going to quit playing kickball, and somebody said, "On what 'bases'?"

I was going to quit playing basketball, and somebody said, "That's foul!"

I was going to quit playing golf, and somebody said, "What fore?"

I was going to quit playing baseball, and somebody said, "You batter not!"

Acknowledgements

A special thank you to those who helped shape this book. First and foremost, God. Without Him I can do nothing. Thank you, Dolores Smith, my late mom, who always inspired me to be great. Danita Smith, my wife, who always supported my decision to write. Shericka Smith, my daughter, who inspires me every day. Bennie J, Bonita, and Clarence Smith, my siblings, who know and love me. All of my extended family, who enjoy me, whether I am funny or not. Facebook friends who enjoy and appreciate my humor. Monique D. Mensah, the principal and founder of Make Your Mark Publishing Solutions, whose professionalism, patience, and guidance allowed me to turn my dream into a reality. Mr. Randy Gray, my talented illustrator. A special thank you to Mr. JaKobi McPherson and Mr. Orlando Jerquan Smith for their artistic submissions for the cover art. And I want to thank me, of course! LOL!

I love you all!
Smitty

By Jakobi McPherson

By Orlando Jerquan Smith

Thank you for reading
For a Pun Time Call Smitty
If you enjoyed the puns, please
leave an online review.

KEEP IN TOUCH WITH SMITTY

Website: www.jokewithsmitty.com
Facebook: Tim Smitty Smith
Instagram: @smittyman1
Twitter: @TimSmit05898602

www.ingramcontent.com/pod-product-compliance
Lightning Source LLC
Chambersburg PA
CBHW021412290426
44108CB00010B/492